The Great Unrest

D1565631

# The Great Unrest

John Brandi

WHITE PINE PRESS / BUFFALO, NEW YORK

White Pine Press
PO Box 236
Buffalo, NY 14201
www.whitepine.org

The author wishes to acknowledge the publishers who first brought the following
poems into print: "Wishing for Rain" - Tangram Press, Berkeley. "Wijiji" - Press
at the Palace of the Governors, Santa Fe. "Spring Fever," "Cosmology," "A Dark
Wood Rhyme," "Terra Nova," - South Asian Ensemble, Canada/India. "Hands
Up" - *5th Overthrowing Capitalism Anthology*, San Francisco. "Theater on the Rails,"
"Among the Ruins," "Einstein's Theory on Happy Living," "Paradise Undone,"
"Diver as Sojourner" - *Venus Rising*, Glasgow.

Publication of this book was made possible, in part, by public funds from the
New York State Council on the Arts with the support of Governor Andrew M.
Cuomo and the New York State Legislature, a State Agency.

Title page drawing: Copy of *Sirena Bicaudata*, a 12th-century mosaic on the floor
of Cattedrale d'Annunzio, Otranto, Italy.

Printed and bound in the United States of America.

ISBN 978-1-945680-29-8

Library of Congress number 2018947145

Good deep
keel about you, strong Edge
sharp as the Sky

a fine balance
for the deepest
waters.

*The world is not with us enough.*
*O taste and see—*

Denise Levertov


*to feel again the uncreated Eros*
*filling my breast,*
*and to be to all, to things near and far away,*
*as the wind's sound and breath.*

Angelos Sikelianos

# Contents

The Great Unrest

18 JUNiD:  (MOON ALREADY set behind cough-jagged tangle of CLiFFS)
2018

50 Years
in/out
these
bare-boned Canyons, WALKing
stick Polished with
a million-dollar Sheen

Sun
upside Down
as I bend to
Tie A ShoE...

# Hiking Stone Mountain Trail

Fifty years
up these slopes, in & out
bareboned canyons

Walking stick lacquered
        with a million-dollar sheen

Mercury sailing through
high-altitude blue

Life
perfectly still, moving
before the eye

Sun upside down
        as I bend to tie a shoe.

## Stealing the Fruit

Cold morning.
Sit down to work, warm my hands
under my legs—

Get in the mode
watching coyote slip under the gate
eyeing fallen apples.

The song I'd sing
soft, uproarious, bush burning
stilled in the breeze

Must be a slip through the gate
like coyote, stealing the fruit
that sends me.

Floating with the Current


"What wonder to be where you are
and know it," Joanne writes.

To let the path end
right where you stop, find yourself
at center, snowgeese circling,
          sunlight flooding the plain.

A place where mountains rise,
valleys sink, and shadows move
                    in uncertain light,

where, just out the door
the brink of something irregular
is exposed: rugged, undefined
          —time, without
                    its usual frame.

A knife-sharp butte on the horizon
growing thinner in the wind . . .

The weightless curve
of the river, deepening the gorge . . .

How imagination gathers,
fills the pail with moonlight
then leaves you
          to the place itself,
          what holds you.

## Wishing for Rain

The long stretch of fields . . .
apricot dazzle where the sun has set.

Go in, close the door, let the moon
fill my glass through the window.

I'd like rain tonight
I'd like sails!

Want the songbirds back
under the eaves, frogs up from
their inside-out galaxies.
        I need those reminders—

Need the spring rain
        a clear and secret rap
from the upper Realm
          just to know
          I'm really cranking.

Bright No Cloud Day

My age spots
have vanished, look at them go!

Off seeding the Journey
          with better understanding
Off decorating the sundial
          with fluttering *hosannas*

Called by the swoon
of the horizon, into the Bardo realm
of the dead, who know Time
          is finally on their side.

No earth-shaking message,
yet here it is on a bright no-cloud day
like shavings of fool's gold
cupped in
          heaven's air.

# Wijiji

Each step over the land is a step inside. While tiny lemon-colored flowers underfoot nod to each other, I roll a pebble under my tongue, speak to stone, decode the calls of canyon wren and thrush. A cliff edge rises, breathes with electrons, ebbs with tidal waltz. What's solid isn't stone, only a severed window of sky where we find hold. The body is brittle air, sunlight, and blood; the universe a mineral-varnished alcove carved with petroglyphs: spiral, solar flare, dot-inside-circle, river-rippled memory path, a game animal traveling beyond the limits of the imagination. We live in and wander through geography that beckons with symbols for another reality. Past and future don't work so well here. The land, the shape of ourselves in it, is circular. Timeless. That's what the rocks say. Following the ranger's map, I seem to be walking a straight line to the ancient site of Wijiji. But no, this is a diaphanous trail, woven into the zodiac itself. Breathe it in, breathe it out. A thousand years ago, the brochures don't tell you, is today.

*Chaco Canyon, New Mexico*

each
step over
the Land,
a step inside; the Body~
                brittle air
                Sunlight
                & Blood.

                The Uni-
                verse
                a mineral-
                Varnished
                Alcove
                carved with
                Petroglyphs...
        The trail?
        ~Diaphanous...
        woven into
        the Zodiac
        itself.

## Hiking the Narrows

I'm ridding myself
of thought I tell her

        Good idea
        she says.

## Spring Fever

Last night, nausea-dizzy
about to convulse, I fell to the floor.

That's it, I thought.
Might never come back.

My spine's weary
even though I've lightened the load.

I'm tired of the times,
often woozy with dull shake.

Could easily tumble over the Great Divide
receive my accolades unnoticed.

On the other hand
if I were out hoeing my corn patch
under a perfect high-noon sky

Or following
the soft wingbeat of an owl
on a clear November night

It could happen
         no better way.

# Happy Hour

Almost ninety today,
twenty degrees cooler inside our adobe walls.
I'll try potting the sun-wilted petunias
and moving them to half shade.

Working in cool lilac twilight
is to recover enzyme lightness—
carbon, chlorophyll, languid planet light.

The trowel weighs nothing in my hand.
A passing cloud dangles a shredded filament
as if to offer a ride.

Head lifts with earth song.
Feet straddle a threshold between
quinine blue and pale almond.

Slowly, it all goes.

The melons give up their heat for sleep.
A crow readies for nightshift.
High peaks turn ruby.

When finally I come back to myself,
to the last of the chores —dishes to wash,
counter to clean, upstairs to open and air,

I feel I've been gone a long, long time.
Turning soil, rolling stones,
unearthing gold in the holy land.

## Inking the Brush

Moon drifts near, over the stream. Daybreak finds it gone, replaced by a sunburst of peaks bowing into the water. Splash my face in the current, watch the flow become divided by a single boulder, regain shape as a spiraling vortex. Boil a coffee, set out pigments, rinse brush in snowmelt, load the hairs with ink, draw them across the page. Liquid vortices trail out, dry into a musical score. Bubbles, flecks of carbon, beads of light, braids of ink: the water's rhythm. And that of heaven: the Milky Way with all its capillary blinks flowing through the cosmos. Ebb, curl, chime, thummp, tingg. Each curve and aberration of the river's shore gives the water new form and timbre. Now a wave, a languid shallow, a torrent spinning with pollen, a mud-sucking bog. River as time line: the course of life, water moving faster in the middle than at the edges.

*Río Conejos, Southern Rockies*

# Cosmology

*The keeper of the cherry blossoms*
*becomes compost for the trees*
— Utsu

Perhaps the secret of the afterworld
is as obvious as the moon backlighting
Hiroshige's flowering plums.

Every metaphor brings us closer
to our own fantasy. No kidding—
we can't escape ourselves.

The stream of life, just a breeze
among the lotus, a slight shimmer
around Cézanne's apple.

One day no more rising
or sleeping, just an inaudible wind
through the window.

Sun no longer warms
Moon no longer cools

and the plums in their bowl
draw you deep between the darkness
of their purple.

# For Sure

Looked into the cosmos last night
saw a great armrest I could lean on.
Nothing to do with the Bull
the Lion  the Swan  the Twins.
Instead, whorled from the great altar
of night, a soft Byzantine couch
where I could lay my unsimple head,
the gray matter of docu-dramas,
botched perceptions
of them and us

and just get back to
self as no self, particles
of anti-matter dancing in the mirror,
an optical illusion
for sure.

# What the Rain Brings

Over the juniper-spotted hills boils a deep violet sky, foreboding yet inviting. A sizzle of white light, a boom, a teeth-clenching rumble shakes the body inside out. Thick splats of rain pound the roof. I hold a glass under the eave and drink right from the sky. At dusk the air clears, a coppery glow bathes the garden paths. Wet stones gleam with iron-oxide patterns that resemble aerial views of the terrain they were plucked from. Willows drip, sunflowers are tall with vigor. Kuan Yin stands erect on a plinth among waving grass inside an oval of river stones—an oval like Sister Bernadette drew on the blackboard for our third-grade class. "This is a picture of your soul," she said, chalking it in. "The soul filled with grace after you were baptized." Then she erased the white, leaving only the black chalkboard. "And this is the soul you had before you were baptized." She described Adam and Eve in the Garden (I thought of my dad's rows of carrots), their sin of disobedience, and the 'stain' we inherited. These days, darkness has no room in my soul. Better, the oval before me: a rain-cleansed garden filled with white cosmos and a dozen bright tomatoes ripening under Kuan Yin.

# At Smiley's

We were all there that evening
We are not there now.

We had no perfect wisdom
Didn't always get it right.

We tried coming
as close to Truth as possible.

Whispering, hammering
lighting the sunken path.

Lifting the anchor, dropping the gown
flashing luck from our sleeves.

Some made off with others.
Some died at their typewriters.

One locked his door with a gun.
Some completed the steps to Nirvana

Some fly with the puffins
off the Farallon Islands.

Some make the rounds, rock
to rock, water to wine, being
to non-being.

That's one aspect
of consciousness.

*Bolinas, California*

# Tell It Straight

Steve was always giving me his tried-and-true rabbi advice cloaked in good, basic zen: theory and practice related to money, marriage, other men's wives, women too young to be lovers, plumbing, automobiles—and health. "Always tell your doctor exactly what's going on when asked. Don't leave anything out." Advice I did not follow when my urologist asked how often I got up at night, and, on a scale of one to ten, what was the strength of my stream. Years later, when things took a downturn, I decided to call Steve, but he was too ill to give counsel. Months later, at his memorial, I drank, recalled good times, shook hands with old friends, then wandered into the woods to say a prayer and take a whiz. The prayer came, but not the whiz. Blocked bladder, muscles unable to relax, followed by thirty-three hours of misery: the drive down the mountain to Sacramento, the wait for my plane, a delay in Denver, a hair-raising ride to the Española hospital, a catheter-induced dam-busting surge of urine. And, seven days of recovery. "Tell it straight, you'll never have a problem." Steve's good counsel. The advice I was too shy, or too stubborn, or both, to follow.

# Stories My Mother Read

Bees disappearing
into a magnolia blossom

Ships upon a marbled sea
after the sun had left the sky

Fairies surely copulating
in nooks of crystal honeycombs

Black cypress cocked with rain
under the twinkling road of the Milky Way

John Silver, Kitty Fisher,
the bells of St. Ann, Mistress Mary

Quite contrary, Captain Bones
and Old Pew

I'd eat white strawberries
in the chimney corner, dream of Polly Flinders

Say take it off again, cure my eyes
while mother read puddings and pies.

# The Panhandle Poetry Club

I was invited to a poetry club
in a small town set among cattle yards
and thorn bramble, a flat sort of place,
evenly cropped lawns, a church
on every other block.

The president began the meeting
with a pledge and a prayer, then turned
it over to the secretary who read the minutes,
mostly about the Panhandle Club's last reading
at Long John Silver's.

The treasurer spoke next, explaining
that club members needed badges
to let the community know exactly who they were.
A small plastic ice-bucket with a Motel 6 logo
made the rounds for contributions.

The club had no women members.
They had tried, the president said, but women
were busy in their houses. Besides, women
had circles, men had clubs.

Then it was talk time.
One man said he had nineteen poems out
and was waiting for replies. Another shared
a letter he sent to an editor who rejected him:

Dear Sir:

Perhaps I mistakenly sent you an early
unfinalized draft of my poem *Dreams Long Ago*.

I am thus enclosing the revised version. Please reconsider
it for publication in your exceptional journal. Do note
that the poem has gleaned honorable mention
in our local newspaper.

Club members nodded
and the president called for reading of new work.
Poems were not to be criticized, he said.
Poets could refer to passages of scripture to help explain
their poems if difficulties or misunderstandings
arose in interpreting them.

A slow, thick evening it was.
Across the table, a young woman
new to the community was sitting in for the first time,
head bowed, a look on her face somewhere between
disbelief and rage.

No poets in crisis here, only confident masters.
With plenty of pomp, these guys wrote steady and clear,
no chaos, no burning explosion of blood,
no need to shake the world upside down with doubt.

It was all a matter of strict meter
and straight corners to be turned with evenly-timed steps.
Truly, they were in top form, and by the next meeting
they all would have their badges.

The last thing I recall was the newcomer
edging closer to the exit, as the men went on and on,
an empty river in a wide bed of gravel
with no place to go, and no swift dance of water.

For Duke & Louie


Little pearls that plague the mind
Stupidopes of wisdom

Various tried and true kernels
of experience

Moments of bell ringing
clarity

Don't mean a thing
if they ain't got that Swing.

# Advice from Wen-Fu

*See the whole Four Seas*
*in the single blink of an eye*
                              —Lu Chi

If it's clever, toss it
If it's hip, crumple it up

If the trail's steep
step with your breath
not yr feet

If you're on the right track
get on the wrong one

If no room to fall
undo yr belt at the edge
of the wall.

If standing tall
get low, lose yourself
in blooming weeds.

## Nanao's Tale

Nanao and I were driving the high desert
out toward Muley Point, when a flaming sunset
had him remembering the island of Java
where he once visited the court ruler of Yogyakarta.

"Here," said the king, "try on my hat."
Nanao put it on. Took it off.

"So heavy!" Nanao bantered
and with a smile returned the king his crown.

Years later, inside the walls
of that same royal court, I visited the king
who, with a smile, remembered
two young men:

"One happy with heavy hat.
  One very Japanese, happy with
                just fisherman hat."

# The North Country

A single-engine plane delivers me into the clouds, toward where the Nuyakuk flows into the Nushagak, everything hazed in blowing snow. We cross the tundra, skirting a knife-edged weather front, cockpit growing dark. When a blast of lemony light finally shines, I scan the arctic desert recalling the village I just left, where a group of artists were creating masks of seadrift, feathers, and skin. One woman whispered through her mask mouth: "If this mouth could speak it would say 'the shaman are alive.' In my village the missionaries have banned the shaman. Now it is hard to get to them. They are hiding." As the plane shakes and tilts, glyph-like faces appear in the frozen tundra below. Hollow eyes follow me, mouths whirl out prismed breath. Frothing clouds envelope the plane. We rock and roll until the storm spits us out on a tiny landing strip. Three Yupik fourth graders and a teacher greet me. The sleigh ride to the school turns my nose red. The kids take pity, "You are cold Mr. John, maybe because your nose sticks out so far." Droplets of mist sting my face. I shut my eyes for the rest of the ride. Under my lids come those faces again, phosphorescent shapes, ultra-violet whispers. "The shaman are alive."

*Upper Nushagak, Alaska*

## Return to Nushagak

Wondering
if I should look up Freddie,
he was pretty old when I met him
all those years ago.
He could have . . .

So I go down to the river
where he used to mend his nets
and two Yupik guys
repairing an outboard motor,
when I ask is Freddie
still around,

tip back their caps
and smile, looking off
toward the sea, putting the question
back to me, as one would, having grown
up in a village where no one leaves:

Freddie?
Still around?
Well, where would he go?

# Musing, A Passing Cloud

*We die, and we do not die*
                    —Shunryu Suzuki

In the cold blue
between incoming mares' tails
an idea rides the wind
            and disappears.
People, too.
In they come, out they go.

They don't perish,
they don't kick the bucket. We didn't lose
uncle Jerry, the president
didn't expire, aunt Gertrude didn't
meet her maker—

The handbell dings,
fleas stop breathing, the Void
grinds its teeth—

Clouds scatter, the moon carries on.
Who's to say we don't?

Perhaps father returned
to Napoli, got back to work
in his dad's tailor shop.

And mother, to her German
river town, glass blowers
and opera singers.

People we say have 'passed'
stare through the Dream when
          the clouds break up.

Generations
of falling leaves, mulching
the earth, rising
          into a new Tree.

# Sweating in Alaska

Hunkering down in the sweat lodge with Joe, Calvin, Tivi, and Alex, I knew there'd be a test of some sort. And a few lessons. My first time on the tundra, and these guys excelled at pulling the rug out from under you. We stripped, left our clothes and towels in the antechamber, and ducked low into the steam room—metal drum ingot red, ceiling dripping. "Got the salt, Tivi? We gonna cook some good white meat." They chuckled. So did I. First lesson: humor. Next, a bucket comes around. We each sprinkle water on the drum—loud pops and sizzles. Second lesson: sharing. Heat rising, skin blushing, we crouch low, washrags on shoulders to avert blistering. Third lesson: stillness, the slightest movement will bring a sting. "You keep still on the tundra, John, game come right up to you." Faces hidden in steam, stories begin: wolf, salmon, caribou; the know-it-all Texan hunter who got lost in a blizzard and wasn't found til spring melt off. With these stories comes the fourth lesson: the art of listening.

After sweating, we weasel into the anteroom to put on our clothes. Mine are missing. "Forget where you put them, John?" A few sly chortles. "Maybe the women up to something, we better find out." We jog through thirty-below snow to Bertha Yaqulpak's house where women and girls are waiting with a pot of king-salmon chowder on the stove, warm bread and cranberry ice cream on the counter. I'm the only one in the room naked, save for the tiny washrag I've covered myself with. The ladies laugh so hard their bellies roll. Their daughters, who I begin classes with tomorrow, cover their mouths and giggle. Next to the chowder, I see my clothes, neatly folded on a warm bath towel—much nicer than my skimpy travel rag. Fifth lesson: humility, acceptance. The women set out spoons and bowls and prepare to sweat. As they leave, one of their 7th-grade daughters points to the ice cream. "Homemade just for you, we picked those berries ourselves."

## Drifter Bar, Anchorage

Between the Penguins
and the Drifters, the Doo-wops
and Motown
comes the thunderbolt howl
          of Little Richard:

*Well it's Saturday night*
*and I just got paid, I'm a fool about*
*my money, don't try to save—*

Used to sing that song
all the time. Fifty years later
here I am   —Saturday night

Just got paid
I'm a fool about my money
never tried to save.

# Looking West, Garrapata Ridge

*for Dennis & Elaine*

You've seen her
in so many places—
      had me looking, too

And there she was
from yr cabin door
      a faint rosy sea haze
filling
that distant narrow cleft
      that holds the moment
before night, the Far East glow
banked by redwoods
      we lift our wine cups to.

Kuan Yin!

borne from limitless Ocean
dancing up the canyon
      on the Wind.

*Big Sur, California*

# Taking Up the Pen, Midnight

*for John Nichols*

Who needs eyeshade
Who needs lamp?

Lift pen,
let ink swim the high tide.

One good line, you're ready
for an all-night run.

When dawn comes,
let the pen sleep, follow deer trails
into the sun.

# This Morning

the ground walks
       beneath my feet

a spirit gives sway
to the tree

water
lifts from stream

Yesterday
moves ahead of me
       —endless banner
of Light

Muse, Madonna
       —her beauty

nothing
       to hide.

Love in the Back Country

Eros wore daffodils, lay naked
on the rocks

In the reeds, by the creek
deer antlered, sun cloaked

Eros filled the jug, poured the wine
brought the fire high

Until the wind howled
and the soft calligraphy of her mane

Turned brittle
in the clench of night.

Eros plucked the goose,
fingers black, fire low

Held out an olive branch
and drank a toast.

Eros tamped a new round
of smoke in her pipe

Put down her song
removed her headband

Stepped out of her sandals
in another land.

# Listening to Bird

Hummingbird
tickles my nose with her tail.
Phonograph needle
drops into polyurethane groove.

Rust climbs the barn-door hinge.
Evening star burns
on the tip of the tongue.

Toes tap-dance
across the kitchen floor.
Moonflower unspirals
to C Jam Blues.

Take it higher, Charlie
       suspend me in the enduring
           Unknown.

## Poetry in Hell's Kitchen

*for Anne & Tom*

Who can forget that night
in Hell's Kitchen, small upstairs
brick auditorium, free beer and wine
in the foyer, the crowd eager, looped,
buying books, psyched.

We all read, shirttails flying,
broom on the nose, trusses
undone, sparks from our heels,
elastic wings madly shuddering,
audience raving, people lifting their arms,
calling out to Jesus, heckling,
waving hankies, tossing money,
standing on their heads
      —completely engaged
          not a silent soul among them.

That kind of a night!
One a good education doesn't prepare
you for, one tugging on the reins
ready to be delivered into the holy nest,
up from the underworld
      waiting to claim Creation,
like Dante in exile
looking back
through the wrong end
      of the telescope.

# On Feet of Gold

*in memory, Ira Cohen*

Every time you played
conspirator and wrung your cape
in the wind, sparks flew.

You were the best-dressed look-alike
to slip through the turnstile
into the subway of Immortality.

The backwards stumble
out the door others mistook for a fall
was a moment of lift off.

The raven on your shoulder
portrayed not gloom, but crooned a steady
scale of unending light.

You wrote to encapsulate
a moment of snapping cameras
inside one's own slapstick delirium,

a human wave coiling into
a superior curve. The Jaguar Priest,
the Taos Clown holding court

in the Church of Holy Innocence.
The shaman, the card player, the voyeur
in creaking shoes—

They traveled with you
as you crossed the yellow police tape
into the blinking lights

of the Caution Zone, jaywalking
as always, the intersection of Great Longing
on feet of Gold.

Today's Weather

Last night
Mars cast a yellow blush,
the village church
got down on its knees.

This morning
rocks are silent, rain's in store.

Let's go back to bed
plant some seeds, regain a little faith
as milkweed explodes
with Prophecy.

# Neighbors

His axe
then my axe
My axe
then his.

# Going for Water

*for RCG*

Under peaks
of snowswirled
       gold, I go

for water, not certain
of tomorrow's waking,
but where the Journey's taken us
     that I do know

You in my arms
      light pouring over
the Rim of the world.

# Gathering Wood

Everywhere you look
lots of snakes
in their holes.

Lots of snakes
in the White
House, too.

*El Rito, NM, 2017*

## Sunrise, Ghost Ranch

Warmest year
on record

And the coldest time
in the hearts
of men.

# Etta at the Line Camp

O, what you done to us
kickin heels
grindin bellies, spashin sweat
in this August heat.

*Jesus God Almighty!*

You don't sing
like that less you brought up
      in a choir
kickin ass
for the Lord.

*Pojoaque, New Mexico*

# Hoisting the Anchor

*—with a line from Etel Adnan*

Exuberant curiosity,
　　　let that steer the course!

Relentless pursuit through false barriers
into the heart of Delight.

Lyrical sojourning—
(silver fragrance
　　　from the heels of the gods.

Active seeking, active learning—
(insight, ideas
　　　up from under.

Sustained inventory
　　　of psychic meanderings.

Open-eyed in every place
and possibility to C A M A R A D E R I E.

Lift a Satchmo streetcorner horn
(inform the living
　　　that they aren't yet dead.

Join a table of strangers
or sit with the desert wind, alone
　　　between lengthening shadows

Always
the convivial Feast!

# Theater on the Rails

At a tiny rural stop, a woman climbs aboard the Malabar Express selling homemade halwa, followed by a girl offering bananas from a platter on her head. A peddler leaves a paperback of Tagore's poems in a stack of books he's put on the seat for my perusal, then walks the aisle dispersing more of the same from a zinc suitcase. Next seat over a man opens the India Times to a post-operative patient's 260 kidney stones spread like coffee beans on a plate. There is a Mr. Praktesh, too, self introduced as "screw specialist." He naps, head resting on a briefcase he earlier opened to rows of nuts, bolts, washers, and a pair of neatly-folded briefs. At a station signed ALIGHT HERE FOR KADAMPUZHA TEMPLE, a bard wearing a sari dyed with good-luck swastikas jumps on, thumps a drum, shakes her bangles, and wails a Bollywood hit.

In this theater on the rails you melt into another, ego leveled, inner eye awakened. Spectator as participant, everyone an actor: farmer, chai wallah, floorsweeper, suit-and-tie barrister, matronly grandma, half-naked sadhu. For an extended instant their stories are yours. You need only yield, smile, come eye-to-eye without notions of them and me. With a loose wag of the head, the play begins. Nothing formulated. Each monologue, every abstraction given value. Each actor sketches a private drama, brings chaos to climax, or leaves the unimaginably weird dangling. The next stop reads OLAPPEEDIKA. Only monkeys line the platform. As the train rolls up, they prepare to board. I was going to get off here, but I believe I'll stay on.

*Kerala, India*

# Paradise Undone

Zhaoxing. The oldest, largest Dong village in China, tucked into a valley edged with forested hills, backed by rice paddies fingering emerald green into a narrow canyon. A river runs out, spanned by fairy-like wooden bridges, fronted by pagodas rising above alleys whose cobble is worked into fish and flower designs. I'm here to shake off the toil of travel, and for awhile my rustic inn is paradise—until a party of chain-smoking, glass-clinking Chinese officials arrives. Babbling in all-at-once loud talk, these suit-and-tie honchos have come to promote tourism. After dark, they hire a local troupe to perform. In traditional dress, dancers and musicians assemble in the square, their songs, pipe playing, and choreography exquisite. But they are repeatedly interrupted by the officials who, loaded to the gills, clap, flash cameras, and gyrate onto the stage. "Welcome to our China!" one yells, glassy-eyed in my direction, while patting a female dancer on the head. Clearly these guys aren't here for the good of Zhaoxing, but for the good of China—and for their wallets. Soon flashy hotels will line the square. And, under bright lights, perhaps the village troupe will be cooerced into versions of Michael Jackson and Beyoncé.

A week later when it's finally time to move on, I board the bus humming a valse triste, a dirge I find myself singing more and more in this world where tourism spoils the rhythm of rural hamlets. The bumpy track out of Zhaoxing quickly becomes a superhighway delivering me into a surreal Babylonian coal haze: rows of quick-love motels, neon gambling dens, go-go girls in slapdash bars built gold-rush style on bulldozed hills. Nope, not worth a valse triste. Better, the songs of the Zhaoxing villagers. Their attention to hard work and festivity. A balance fine-tuned through wisdom and tradition—the art of staying in place.

*Guizhou Province, China*
*2003*

59

# Toward the Summit, Above the Haze

Mountains disobey
all commands, rise above human pride,
feuds of opinion, the cuckold,
seductress, glorified plagiarisms,
           the sin of perfection.

The walking stick has no place
in pompous humdrum, the bog
of money making, relentless contour
of another war.

A cloud passes, cherub pink.
Aerial, innocent, it floats over human drama
      —an uncompromised rendezvous.
No herd, no flock, no gaggle.

An honored hero,
speaker of silence
        sailing on its own.

*Serra Dolcedormo*
*Basilicata, Italy*

Terra Nova

The horizon, undone.
A bodice of butterflies,
                heather and pine.

No track of another, no trace.
The trail loops upward
over pebbled streams, into the arc
of a circling hawk.

Above beech, chestnut, oak
thin ribbons of road, carts, taverns,
the greasing of axels, and today's purchase
of oil and flour,

a cobalt sky bends
to meet a band of fossil rock
      —home of Apollo's sunbeams
veins of melancholy
                salt of poetry.


*Monte Pollino, Italy*

# Among the Ruins

The tour-bus crowd has moved on. Parasols, retro skirts, oiled boots, floppy hats, butt-hugging shorts, purple hydration packs. Some plugged in, some checking cellphone reception, some talking real estate, politics, divorce, weight-loss programs. Listing travels (where from, where next), they parade over the hill leaving puffs of dust, soap scent, silence. Tender and melancholy, the land quivers. Damp hills rise into mist, dark ravines cut toward the sea. On a flower-carpeted knoll the Temple of Segesta gives a pearl gleam. No roof, only sky. No walls, just columns; through them a wind-harp breeze from the far shine of the Tyrrhenian Sea. The site marks an auspicious intersection of grassy coves and marly outcrops, a true harbor for the gods. Light dances in ponds, sun-heated fennel fills the nose. On the missing altar, I place a softly-sculpted stone—a warm, humid-to-the-touch amulet. Perhaps it will lure Athena, keen-eyed and wise, to revive the human race. Maybe Herakles will answer. Or Durga, a weapon in each hand to slay the tyrants who plunder the earth and cover their rape with lies. Humans have reached a cul-de-sac of no return. Either we step aside to let earth repair herself, or ingest a double shot of hemlock and call it quits.

*Segesta, 425 BC, Sicily*

Tender & Melancholy..
the Land Quivers..

Tempio
di Segesta.
Sicilia
(2016)

NO WALLS,
& Just columns &
& between them,
aloft from the
Tyrrhenian Sea...
A wind-harp
Breeze...

## Hello, Hello

Hello hello
dark-eyed junco, purple
          prairie clover
tiny withered-up scroll
          of snakeskin

It's autumn.
Once again, life's ending
just in time, too—

Things have gotten so bad
          one can no longer
          pretend it's green.

# Einstein's Theory on Happy Living

Today the news reports that Einstein's *Theory on Happy Living* was auctioned off for 1.5 million dollars. But it won't cost millions to find happy living on your own. Stand on a derelict ship and do a wave-slap drop over the prow into a rough-tumble port of call. Excellent territory to shake off the waters of lineal humdrum and get back to the joy of the indefinable. No passport, nothing pre-planned, nobody waiting at the airport flashing your name. I lay aside the news and return to Shirley Hazzard's *Ancient Shore: dispatches from Naples*:

*Those who have never experienced solitude in a strange and complex place—never arrived in the unknown without credentials, without introductions to the right people, or the wrong ones—have missed an exigent luxury. Never to have passed those austere evenings on which all the world but oneself has destination and companion, is perhaps never to have felt the full presence of the unfamiliar.*

Happy Living? Go slow. Go without a moan. Go with determined independence. Go beneath the Deep they schooled you in, the waters they claimed had a bottom. What accomplishments have we, stirring about the surface, no pitfall, no dangle over the abyss, no gaping maw of doubt and curiosity?

Under Vesuvio

David, Steve, Leonard, Mose,
Stephanie, Joanne got away, ducked
the doom, rode the slow expanding
ripples across the pond.

He didn't say I can see the light
at the end of the tunnel, he said I can see
the light on the *other side* of the tunnel.

She wasn't specific about any *far shore*.
Instead she looked to the 'topographical
enlightenment swooning in the back yard'
and called it the *timeless shore*.

He never mentioned dying. Simply
opened his fingers and let a few grains
of turquoise sift into the air.

She didn't add her name to the ocean
of all endings. Instead, she lay me on a pyre
and removed her clothes.

Today, above rivers of fire,
on the black slopes of Vesuvio,
green blades of grass meet the sunrise
under a passing cloud.

*24.9.17, Pompeii*

# Diver as Sojourner

On the lid of an excavated Greek tomb, a naked diver is poised in mid air, suspended between mortality and immortality, about to plunge into a pale azurite sea. His body, given a hematite hue, is that of a sun-tanned  athlete trained in the outdoors. Fit for his metaphysical journey, he will swim the underworld, sustained by a gift of honey from his relatives. The twin columns from which he has leaped might represent the Pillars of Herakles that once marked the edge of the known world. The painting is a narrative for the dead—and for the living. Diver as sojourner, the resolute explorer of curious mind and eager heart, poised, with a push from the wind, above a sea of undocumented mystery. A liquid world where the bardic paddle answers the Siren's call and sets one forward on an ir-reversible course through time and transformation.

*Poseidonia / Magna Graecia*
*South Italy*

## Plein Air

On the Corso
hide and seek goddesses
stroll the lordly warmth of Napoli,
designer shades, net leggings, volume bras.

Where to set my easel?

On Toledo?
Next to Virgil, in red plastic specs
and silver shoes, dressed to retire
into the scheme of intrigue,

sick of snobs and dandies,
bookworms, wish they weres
and wanna bes.

Where to unwrap my colored pencils?

Above the catacombs
on the streets of the old acropolis
among flatfoot Romans

leaving the Temple of Echoes
for the unprincipled
human parade?

Lovely orbs of cosmic
dust. Flurry of legs, baggy cuffs
skin-tight skirts—

Where to attach my eye?

Should I court a prolonged kiss,
dribble squid ink on expensive vellum,
test my non success jumping rope
with Little Helen of Troy?

Better to unfold
my three-legged stool, paint unrivalled
strokes of breath and death
and undemanding skies,

set out my alms bowl
in case some passing king
happens by.

Where to fix my gaze?

On Diana, Laxmi, Hera
their unwrinkled features on display
in the public market?

I'm having trouble getting started.

Perhaps I'll take my brush
to the glowworms in the foliage,
crusty skulls of learning

buried under the altar
where Santa Patrizia's blood liquefies
every Tuesday after Mass.

Plein air painting—

in the heart of Napoli
beneath the vibrating windows
of lovers going up and down

behind half-closed curtains
over Doña Zaza's al gusto
Delicatessen.

It's time to get out
my soft-lead Palomino #2,
scratch a narrative iambic

go for broke
lay down with the great granddaughter
of Emperor Augustus

become the center
of controversy.

Should I claim my praise,
squeeze a tube of lampblack
between the fingers of the pickpocket?

Buy a ricotta pie from the nun
guarding San Gregorio's
famous bone?

Splash a dollop of Ionian yellow
and paint the soccer shouts?

maybe a sweet amber glaze
for the Venus of Rags on the steps
of the public treasury?

What shape of color
for these children running free?
little saplings,
          tiny lambs' ankles

mafia fathers with dark ties
waving kerchiefs
from gold-wheel limousines?

Plein air—

Out among the hungry
and the longing, the bigbottomed
and the strong

A dusty outcast
in a river of sun, painter
of gilded limbs, Delphic doublecross

      an anonymous brush
where the ships come in.


*Porta Nolana, Napoli*

25 SeTremBre
WAPoLi: Sipping
Wine in the CloiSterS

I bare my heart
offer my FLOWeRS
open my Book
Scan My EYE
SpreaD my Wings
Straighten the
altaR CLOTH...
I fold my Lapel
FLame the Wick
bow to the infant
unRobe the Virgin
Be-heAD
my HeaD...
I peel away the Gold
thrum my string
Relieve the Chalice
Smooth the Linen
Sever the Tie
ask foR a Relic
Pray for my Twin...
$ * I Soften my Stance
Divine the Syllables
of my aDventuRous foreBears
- Tune my GLANCe.

# People on a Train

Nun in gray,
breast flattened under white bib.

Big man
reading little book.

Vagabond,
his idea of space.

Each reflected
on my window, over passing cypress
stony fields, rows of olives.

And the angel
mute as a bluebird, across the aisle?
For her I'd undo myself

from the passing scenery
turn to her,
relax

smell the frost in the air,
erase my face
in hers.

*La Frecciabianca*
*Trinitapoli - Caserta, Italy*

# A Slow Amble

Did I miss out by not taking the overnight ferry from Napoli to Palermo? Arriving by sea would have let the island reveal its pleasures in the slow unveiling of dawn. Instead, tales of claustrophobic cabins and diesel fumes swayed me onto a one-hour flight. Comfortable, quick, perhaps too quick. In 1787 Goethe arrived in Palermo by ship, sun bolting across the city, mountains rising behind, headlands stretching away, foliage swaying like vegetal glowworms. "Instead of hurrying impatiently ashore, we remained on deck until driven off. It might be long before we could again enjoy such a treat for the eyes from such a vantage point."

How rare to enter the unknown with a slow savoring, as in sniffing a glass of Nero d'Avola before drinking; or giving Botticelli's *Allegory of Spring* proper foreplay to heighten one's craving. A new land needs to give you a look, send out its pheromones, elicit an erotic pull—each contour, swell, and curve reeling you in. Gangplank down, you find way to the mercati, ancient paving underfoot, new lingo in the ear: jazz-riff opera, bebop banter, a melodic ring. Neurons flare, ears and eyes go drunk. Sawed-off heads of swordfish point heavenward from a fishmonger's counter—his wife displaying a necklace of giant octopus tentacles. Today, no familiar text, tempo, constrictive habits. Just a slow amble. Trace the hand along stone, smell garlic roasting in a kitchen, halt to buy bread and olives. Stop for a coffee, maybe ask for a place to lay the head. The barista, her gypsy darkness against the lemon-colored walls, lets her eyes burn through you as she sets down a demitasse of espresso. Like a strong hit of grappa, you  lose balance, then come clear. With great precision you'll remember her, and forget the directions.

# Spaccanapoli

The Old Quarter—
strung with drying sheets
pulleys of wet nightgowns, the cloak
of Wonder Woman soaking
              with Jupiter's longjohns.

Steam from the Roman
baths, wild action
in the catacombs   —bullet holes
        above dripping laundry.

"I suggest we go out
        and make love on a clothesline"

Sure.

Over passing theologians
and sleeping Persephones, dutiful beekeepers
and the church of Saint Mary the Pure

Let me throw you Down!
Hips to floor, pillowed firm

Tongue, spurs    —come Near!
let the organ sound
the bells go off, the cup be filled
              before a walk around town.

*Decumano Maggiore, Napoli*

75

## Kneeling with the Penitents

You enter the church under a stone lintel carved with humans danc-
ing arm-in-arm beneath priests raising crosiers and chalices. Over
the altar, a painting so aged and smoke darkened as to refuse all
meaning. Slowly appears a martyr holding two severed breasts on a
plate. Before her the infirm are rolled into place, prayer heavy,
slumped in wheelchairs. Behind kneel shadowy figures, each lost in
penitent haze. One tears at her hair, begging atonement for infideli-
ties. One pounds his chest, confessing lies and treacheries. One ad-
justs a hearing aid, rolls an eye to the prophets on the ceiling,
pummels his brow, and lists the discord he has sown. *Vedi che son un
che piango!* Is it Dante he quotes, begging out of hell's asphyxiating
stench, the blistered bodies that refuse to become ash?

When a ring of noon bells quiets the retch of torment, a sweeter
voice rises. Moderato at first, until from under its veil, it revs
vivacissimo and the listener rides a sea of ascending cries, not un-
like those of lovemaking. The pitch is perfect, climax not far off.
I lower the kneeler and pretend to pray, just to listen, to imagine.
But, instead of carnal pleasure, the ear receives love borne of the
highest heaven. Desire and loss join, body ignites with apocalyp-
tic fervor. One soars on this woman's cries: above earthly rabble,
the blemish of history, the all-judging god praised by the priests
waving clubs over the dancers at the door. As the woman's sighs
fade, a calm afterglow presides. Hair pullers and chest beaters
have silenced their litanies. Downcast mouths are now upturned,
giving way to smiles.

# Drinking with Juno

No better way to spend
an afternoon than drinking
with the likes of Juno,
then falling off
      the earthly stool

into the lap
of some woodland nymph
or into the arms of Sophia
Loren, smiling
      from a poster
      on a sunlit wall:

*Everything I am*
      *I owe to spaghetti*

No better way to greet
the Angel than to discard
      humility's thin disguise
bring myself up from hell

drinking Cinzano
      in the Blue Grotto.

*Piazza Dante, Napoli*

## Leaving Gallipoli

Travel out to go in
shift weight, see who's neighbor
dust off rank.

Refuse the borders
and the bans, the sanctions
and scams.

No fancy travel shirt
aluminum trekking pole
self-inflating head rest.

Try a dhoti, something light
gourd of water, roll of papyrus.
Take the stony road

into the rumpled core
of hidden caves, sea-perched crannies
of the fertility gods.

Go primal
eye to eye, face to face.
Genuine, personal chemistry!

Try on the shoes
of somebody you thought the other.
Disappear for months if you have to.

In the deepest valley
ask where the world begins.
Ever curious, sail the danger.

Be Odysseus
in the churning straits. Return,
not hardened, but wise.

Lift a stone, chisel
a beam, sink in the axe
        and build again.

5 MAY: ARGIROÚPOLIS / CRETE

OMNIA·MVNDI·FVMVS

I bend back a
flowering Bougain
Villea
from a stone gate
& discover, in
chiseled Roman
square capital
lettering, this
"Smoke & Shadow"
inscription

## Omnia Mundi Fumus et Umbra

Five hundred years ago in a Cretan mountain village, a Venetian princess, daughter of feudal lord Francesco da Molin, was engaged to marry the rebel Georgios Kantanaleos. The wedding, initiated by the Kantanaleos family, was intended to reconcile the Venetians and the Cretan insurgents. But Francesco had other plans. During the wedding feast he got Kantanaleos and his men drunk, then called in the army to capture and hang them. His message: rebels, keep to your caves, stay away from our daughters, seek no reconciliation.

At da Molin's ruined villa, I bend back a flowering bougainvillea from a stone gate and find OMNIA MUNDI FUMUS ET UMBRA carved into the lintel: *Everything in the world smoke & shadow.* A warning to the rebels, it also pertained to the victors. In time, the Venetians would fall to the Turks, the Turks to the Greeks. *Smoke and shadow,* yes. All life transient, political power illusion. Today it takes no effort to identify our smoke-and-shadow big mouths. Send them out wearing OMNIA MUNDI FUMUS ET UMBRA dunce caps. Chant the words of Nezahualcoyotl, that wise servant-of-the-people from another era:

> *Could it be true we live on earth?*
> *On earth forever?*
>
> *Even the finest stones begin to split,*
> *even gold is tarnished,*
> *even precious bird plumes*
> *shrivel like a cough.*
>
> *Just one brief instant here.*

*Argyroúpolis, Crete*

81

## Lissos at Dawn

Let the snows
of the Lefká Ori fill the springs
       of Asklepios—

My throat
sweet Claire, is dry.

May fresh rain wash the silt
from buried coins, reveal the face
of Artemis wreathed
       with leaping dolphins.

Let us sing the old songs
over, and with each dawn
       begin the New.

*Sougia, Crete*

V.13 Sfakia Coast
Crete

The Hopi STAR...
the Minoan STAR...
The Ancient Spiral
~Constellations too~
Rising

over the
Lefká Ori...

Ah, to have
floated
a long, long way off
from the Dark of
the Times...into
the Fierce Radiance of the gods!

&
what flowers are these?
expressing mid-gesture GLORY
...sweet upright goldfinch Yellow
(from Blue clefts of Stone).

## Feast of the Transfiguration

Sing me into the orange tree
under the silent bells
of the crumbling monastery.

Deliver me from the wrinkle of darkness
into the fragrant bough
where no clock ticks
        with dying numbers.

I'll spread ripe oranges
in a circle of moonlight,  and wait
by the gleaming sea—

I want to sleep
without book or teacher
        a tiny key in the clasp
           of your Love.

*Agia Paraskevi, Crete*

# Back in the USA

*St Augustine, Tremé, New Orleans*

Goin' down
get a new pair of shoes
Feel the earth
       walk under my feet,

Goin' for
big mountain climbing boots
tapdance heels
take me out of lowland haze

No charade
No fist in my face
No backtalk
       threat of noose.

Goin' sandal me up
like prophets of old, walk high seas
into the holy apothecary
drink jade tea
       from a Chinese jug

Cool my blisters
in Leaves of Grass, get my kicks
rousing rebels
       from the cosmic beat
of unmeasured rhyme

Goin' down
strip off my clothes, walk naked
through the cage, make way
for the Mona Lisa
        headgates

Pack my vocal chords
with honeyed pears, imbibe
my daily dose
        of pagan excitement

Goin' down
        goin' down . . .

Yodel
my ass off where things
are Clear.

Goin' shine
my dancing shoes,
stretch my legs over the melting
glacier, reel in Paradise
before it's too late.

# The Unknown Poet

*in memory, Fred Marchman*

The Supreme Diviner, the omnipotent
transmitter of pure uncompromised creativity
would have him sitting here, the Unknown
Poet, cooling in the stream's flow

after theosophizing his way
through the Big Easy, he with a few cents
to his name, wordsmith by trade
        reed-mat publisher
        scribbler of ultra-sound Equity

no sense of caps
or punctuation, save for the the pixels
on a turtle's back, or the fork marks
in a pie crust.

Throw the covers off,
hand him a wooden pillow and a pipe.
Maybe Virgil's headdress
or the lynx collar of the Jade Princess.

Give him feathers
and a shining robe,
        Give him quiet
and happy pageantry, let him rise
beyond the bards
        who steal the screen.

# A Dark Wood Rhyme

Need to get lost
for a night, go beyond time,
trust the fog that hides the sun.

Need to loosen
boots, rediscover the face of the moon
in an empty spoon

take leave
over the swinging bridge, no map
to lead me back.

The world trembles,
the water is deep. Ice melts in harbors,
dust blows from the sea.

Who for a companion
as I follow this dark wood rhyme,
who of simple mind

will doff the robe
and jump on the cart
for a ride?

## At the Headwaters

Good to the ear
this moon-shadowed roar
of dividing waters.

To wake far from the hard strike
of the human voice, hear the sigh
of creaking spruce,

a rumble
in the Bear's stomach, drum
of the river's surge.

Alone at the headwaters
a hundred peaks, a thousand blooming
moss flowers for neighbors.

27 Enero 2018
(Waitin' for Rain)

Remember when "getting somewhere" was important?

These Days, in the sub- terranean waters of a coral reef...

I'd rather inch along

or go slow-pokin' a ridge of ultra-violet light on a Himalayan Peak: Destination Un-found...

Ah, to lose track, receive ever-clear prophetic whorls, funneling UP from the UNKNOWN!

# Small Truths

*for Joaquin Coyote*

Thanks
for pointing out the emerald eyes
of the wolf spider waiting for the fly
in the wrinkled crease of the elm.

Thanks for hesitant wind,
the airy realm of frigate birds
who rarely touch down.

Thanks for the tangled path
to the Monkey Temple, a round of sakè
at ten thousand feet,

a hand-turned bowl
of spalted beech, table I work on
stool that props me.

Thanks for sunlight
knapped from obsidian, a stone blade
for the veil of darkness, small truths
on which to rise.

*the high track to Osier*
*Tusas Mtns, New Mexico*

## Cortez, Colorado

The Community Believer's House
right next to The Community
Shooter's Club.

Ice plumed stratosphere
above, geese migrating south,
earth rolling below.

Everything in motion.
Folks in town, pickups on the strip,
a night at the movies, holsters on hips.

## Hands Up

Meaning
I am not doing anything
with them,

have no hidden weapon
except the pen
in my pocket.

You can shoot
but you can't down
my angel.

Therefore I stand
to continue.

# Grass Hill Poem

Sit here under a juniper
with a box of Cracker Jacks
until the showers pass

Put into practice the Great Way
before my head
turns gray

A little bit of karma
goes a long way, right up to the top
of Quandary Peak

Break off some bunch grass
sweep it across the page
ink-dipped,
   I've caught the sky!

What was it
old monk Gensei said?

"Deep in poetry musings
I forget to go home."

# The Malpais

look at this fire—

the one they taught
was under purgatory,
big flapping flame
of eternity

the one you'd taste
if you looked up girls' dresses
or danced
with another man.

well blow me
down, matey, it was paradise
all the time
          opiate inspiration
ample motivation
to lift the skirt
of reason.

*Malpais Lava Beds*
*New Mexico*

## What More?

Exquisite, standing there
ringed by mountains, just the new boots
nothing else on, eyes of the daffodils
fluttering a double-blink of awe
perfectly syncopated to each beat
of her heart. What more
this unwrapped
poem pure creature
and force, rise of the breast
warm snow in the musical cleft
as she bends, stretches arms to sky
opulent bloom that feeds each line I write.

## Dust Bowl Daze

First they moved the trade-school
classes—hairdressing, autoshop, weaving
electronics, computer science, adobe making
to a larger college, thirty miles away.
Then the mercantile shut down—bread, milk
tortillas, newspaper, custom-butchered beef.
Next, the gas station: oil change, tire repair
air, battery charge, tune up.

This, after the dance hall, saloon,
local barber, a pottery shop, and a cafe
shut their doors. The town dump closed, too.
Next the glass recyclers gave up.
Now there's talk of busing the schoolkids
elsewhere, maybe even giving up
cattle and sheep—after all
it hasn't rained in six months,
price of hay is climbing, and you can't
pass on ranching to youngsters
uninterested in restoring a fallow field
while the tumbleweeds blow.

Drugs are doing fine, though
along with general depression
and now with the failed snowpack
fields are withered, fire hazard high.
Two homes burned last month, despite
a state-funded fire-hydrant project.
It just so happens there's no pressure
in the line. Water table's dropped,
the aquifer's shot. In the driest counties
some tough-on-times farmers are selling

97

what's left of their water to the oil barons,
who, when they've finished filling their barrels
with what they've fracked, will leave
for our children the haze and poverty
of the Dust Bowl days.

# Sawing Up Aspen

I recall firewood stacked
with a slight inward lean against
a stone house in Sicily.

Along a road laid by Romans
were many such homes, neither prettied up
nor gentrified, simply well maintained —loved
over centuries, and that love, that attention
(to the cobble paving, stone aqueduct,
brush piled for songbirds, the maintenance
of an olive press half hidden
    in a sacred grove)  passed on,
          and on.

These householders
explain themselves better
than kings or presidents, they dig in
don't wear their hearts out
with trivia. A little gossip's ok
     —but so is breathing
        space.

A tourist needs only leave
the Caravaggios and marble altars,
head over the hill, share an old-vine primitivo
with these hands-in-the earth contadinos
who hold high their determination,
    the desire to give back,
       renew.

# Afternoon Reveille

*I sometimes think all is concentrated for me*
*in these hardy yellow-flowered weeds*
                                        —Walt Whitman

Were we of spider
milkweed, or wing, merry
in the Sun's flame,

not staked to waiting angels
nor squeezing dreams
through a bottomless sieve.

All of us derelicts
of the same Song, buds
on one Stem.

The Gardener's surprise—
a sudden wildflower
beauteous among the beans.

Evening Read

Sit back
glance at the rafters
—ah, the stars are shining through!

reach for Borges:
*centuries and centuries and only in the present*
*do things happen*

Akhmatova:
*My verse is my link with time*

Thoreau:
*I find my clothes covered*
   *with young caterpillars these days*

    ◆


Smell the desert out there
   cliffrose and Navajo tea—
woody pulp, bindery glue
smell it, too.

Been a long time
since I've spoken of these.

Spring light
on each page, these deep
   winter hours.

# Morning Read

How books opened randomly
      reveal the state of things—

Herodotus, for example, musing on Egypt's fallen king
Psammetichus:
*that unalterable law of history: whoever elevates himself will be humbled.*
*Be not voracious, do not jostle your way to the fore, maintain moderation*
*and humility; otherwise the chastising hand of Fate, which beheads*
*braggarts and all who preseume to lord over others, will descend upon you.*

Ryszard Kapuscinski:
*Mediocrity is dangerous: when it feels itself threatened*
*it becomes ruthless.*

Wislawa Szymborska:
*When I pronounce the word Future,*
*the first syllable already belongs to the past.*

Jack Kerouac:
*a great humanity is coming . . . but madness will continue to rule*
*in high places, the trick is to get rid of the pride*
*with a conscious loathing of it.*

Adrienne Rich:
*The Beauty of darkness is how it lets you see.*

# Year of the Dog Poem

I'm not sitting here wine-drunk
waiting for Inspiration

Inspiration's already
walked in on its own, stoked the fire
settled onto the rug
       looking up, as if to say
       become a dog
       be genius, dance with thunder
          invent if you have to.

But don't just sit there
feeling the hard notes of anger
       as you open and close
          the news.

Bark, growl, forsake the ruin,
rise from your seat. A cleaner sky
has need of you.

Woof, yodel, yowl
through the raving airwaves.

O bone
O paw, billions upon billions
of crooning galaxies
       make silent the hands
       of our clocks.

*1.1.18*

## Essential Guantanamo

Give me that old time
grassroots dirtfloor elemental swing

A bring-me-up-from-the-docks
downhome Afro pine-for-your-sweetie rhumba
                              —*Hit it!*

Shake your craving hips
roll in the foam—

Loosen eyeballs, shoulders, legs
free the pelvis, unlock the brain waves
                    —*Taste it hot, taste it again!*

Down with the embargo—
Mambo-ize the uptight flock!

Cut the barricade, wrap the plutocrats
with their own red tape

Hat to the wind, party up to the stiffs
who think money is everything
                              —*Ahora Sí!*

Chant down tyrant man
get him low, shuffle slow
                essential Guantanamo.

*Baila!*
let the great impromptu begin!

Santiago de Cuba, 2010

# Rosie's Rap

There he was, fresh off di Royal Sea Dream, strutting
along, hiding his head under a plastic see-through umbrella.
"Sure ting you looking fah Chill Out Bay, mon. You gwan take
di Redemption boat?" (The man he keep his head down).
"Sir, no look away. First I read horoscope fi yuh." (The man
he no lift an eye). So mi guh one way, him guh di oda,
walk a steady walk dun Folly Rd. (The man be movin quick).
Wen di rain stop mi saw him asking di taxi mon
fah Chill Out Bay, iz t-shirt wid a big flag say:

I'LL KEEP MY GUNS, MY GOD
MY COUNTRY, MY RELIGION
MY POLITICS, YOU CAN KEEP
THE CHANGE

Keep de change, uh? I no wurthless sistah.
Me gwan call down dat rain again.

*Search-me-Heart*
*Portland Parish, Jamaica*

# Indian Camps Burning in the Land of the Free

Driving south, hwy 285
from Santa Fe, a sudden roadblock
　　　—overturned propane truck
somewhere down the line.

All traffic rerouted, a 60-mile detour
through Bosque Redondo　—prison camp
for Navajos starved off their land, forced onto
the Long Walk: 300 miles: Fort Defiance, Arizona
　　　　　to New Mexico, winter, 1864.

The detour follows that walk, bumper to bumper
　　　—angry drivers "losing time" (at 70 mph)
on a paved hwy that covers in one hour
　　what the troop-whipped Indians
　　　　　could barely walk in a month.

At the wheel, I ponder America's
scorched-earth Indian wars, when the radio interrupts
with the 5 o'clock news: "Sioux protesters have lost
their battle against the Dakota Pipeline,
　　　　　their camp is burning"

Sand Creek
　　Wounded Knee
　　　　Standing Rock . . .

Indian camps still burning
　　　　in the Land of the Free.

*Fort Sumner, NM, 2016*

# Big, Bigger, Biggest

Bigger biceps
Bigger tits, bigger balls
bigger lips

Bigger automobiles
Bigger pills, bigger asses
Bigger bills

Bigger banks
Bigger soup lines
Bigger shopping carts

Bigger blather
bigger horseshit, bigger trigger
bigger whip

Bigger debt, bigger dam
bigger drought
Bigger slums

Bigger begging bowls
Bigger tax break
for corporate bums

Bigger glove compartment
for the american gun
Bigger sirens, bigger clubs

Bigger missiles
bigger empires, bigger role call
for mercenaries and thugs

Bigger walls
to keep people out
and keep people in

A wall
for my grandkids
and their kids.

Let the walls
fall.

# On Removing Boundaries

Migrating
through cities and hills,
           the fog rolls in.

The illegal moon, alien stars,
the coyote, the desert wind
        set the cobwebs shaking.

Little bracelets
and plastic hair pieces
        keep the alarms ringing.

Madre, niño, abuelo
cuñado, hermana, nieto—
        the bullhorns crackle.

Zapotec, Nahua, Maya
farm worker, meat packer,
housekeeper—
        the handcuffs open.

K'iche', Catracho, Cuzcatleca,
stonemason, cook,
        hotel maid.

Inside the map
of human touch, nobody sleeps
on separate sides.

*People's March against*
*unconstitutional immigration policies.*
*USA, 6.30.18*

## Blue Guitar, Yellow Wave

No wonder our trusty bard left,
he saw the future. Wrote it, sang it,
watched it arrive.

Full tilt. The hydra headed monster
tearing through the curtain.
Of course he bowed out.

No more need—
He lived the Gift, he gave
the Gift.

Sailor of imperial seas
companion of deep shine
bootlegger of the Aegean breeze

Painter of thieves
and banned dreams, now
with his bow unstrung

Behind the veil of asteroid haze
following Marianne
aboard the restless wave.

*Rome, Italy*

## Remembering Joanne

Time to put down the pen
throw open the shutters, welcome her in
           —a dance of pine needles
        on the breeze . . .

Put on some music
        (Oaxaca, Senegal, Barranquilla)
fetch stovewood
        stoke the flame
enjoy jetstream quick flash
connect-the-dots
                COMMUNION

dab of chutney
pinch of herb
sprinkle of unknowing

Unfold a new map
to the Golden Threshold
& let yourself GO
        (like raisins going back to grapes
grass hut to field, Buddha's belly
            a plum tree's burl).

Remember—
    *When the story gets going. Hang on*
Give a deep bow
        for times around a table
            small enough for All.

## Planting Garlic, Late October

Pallid moon
shamelessly bare
        —and the refrigerator, too.

•

Bankrupt world
stocks, mortgage, longterm success
has us tied to the done
        of our own doing.

•

Plant these seeds deep.
In darkness, one more
        victory over madness.

*Río Arriba, New Mexico*

# Every Day Off

Every day off is a day on.

Unbraiding
the skin talk.

Debunking
the evidence

Unsaddling
time from logic.

Everyday a dice throw.

Ball of string
back to the entrance
of the Cave.

# Towards Solstice

*for Renée*

I open the door to your studio
let sunlight fill the house. Everywhere
warmth gushes out    —your presence
every trial, effort, beauty of accomplishment
the very shape of life, your essence
placed over me    —a garland!
Room to room I wear it, dissolved
in your outline as I walk.


*El Rito, New Mexico*

# Notes to the Poems:

*Floating with the Current:*
The quote is from Joanne Kyger.

*Advice from Wen Fu:*
See *Wen Fu* (*The Art of Writing*), a collection of witty pronouncements on literature in the form of prose poetry by Lu Chi (261-303), translated by Sam Hamill (Breitenbush Books, 1987). A version translated by Tony Barnstone and Chou Ping (Shambala, 1996) quotes Lu Chi as saying: "*The poet knocks on silence to make a sound*" followed by Lu Juren: "*Inspiration enters between the border of hard work and laziness.*"

*On Feet of Gold:*
The title pays homage to Ira Cohen's book *On Feet of Gold* (Synergetic Press, 1986).

*Etta at The Line Camp:*
Etta James appeared at The Line Camp in 1982, a bar-dance hall just north of Santa Fe that featured such performers as John Lee Hooker, Taj Mahal, Flaco Jimenez, The Rastafarians, Asleep at the Wheel, and Gatemouth Brown. Opened in 1936, it closed in the late 80s, an intimate, affordable, bawdy, heel-kicking place—the likes of which no longer exists in Santa Fe. Revisiting the premises (now a distillery), I was led to a wall where a framed photograph had captured the very night Etta rocked the house. Among the crowd on the dance floor, I spotted myself, gettin' down.

*Paradise Undone:*
Fifteen years after my visit to Zhaoxing (2003), the town has definitely changed. A few travelers' reports: "An interesting evening show is included in the 100-yuan ticket you must purchase to enter the village." – "A new high-speed train gets you close, and there's a super-fast highway opened recently." – "Most old houses are now souvenir shops or wi-fi cafes spoiled with cute signs." – "2 hours is plenty for a visit, the village isn't as attractive as what travel ads say." – "The Chinese got a large loan from the world bank to expand Zhaoxing for tourism with a huge parking lot, museum, artificial lake, and new buildings made to look traditional." – "I was welcomed with fireworks and a performance, even dined with locals who love to sing and drink." – "Go sooner not later, before hotels are completed for tour groups who come for only a short stay."

*Diver as Sojourner:*
"Pillars of Herakles" (the Strait of Gibraltar). "Sustained by a gift of honey":

among the ambrosias, honey was preferred by ancient Greeks to sustain the departed on the immortal journey. Honey found in excavated Greek tombs has been so well preserved that, even after 3000 years, it retains its liquid form.

*A Slow Amble:*
See *Italian Journey (1786-1788)*, Johann Wolfgang Von Goethe; translated by W.H. Auden and Elizabeth Mayer (North Point Press, 1982). I have paraphrased part of Goethe's descriptions from aboard ship as he arrived in Palermo.

*Omnia Mundi Fumus et Umbra:*
Argyroupolis isn't the only village professing to be the site of the fated wedding. Some leagues west another village lays claim, citing a ruined castle once lived in by Francesco da Molin. A phrase similar to *smoke and shadow*—*"mirrors and smoke"*—was coined during the Watergate scandal by journalist Jimmy Breslin: "All political power is primarily an illusion—mirrors and blue smoke" in reference to President Nixon's fraudulent statements. See, also, Horace: PULVIS ET UMBRA SUMUS (*we are dust and shadow*), p. 360, *Horace: the Odes, Epodes and Carmen Saeculare*, Clifford Herschel Moore, ed.

*Lissos at Dawn:*
Lissos flourished in the Hellenistic, Roman, and First Byzantine periods. It is situated in a remote cove on the south coast of Crete, backed by steep slopes rising into the Lefká Ori, Crete's highest mountains. An ancient spring flows below the ruins of a Greek healing temple dedicated to Asklepios (or Asclepius), god of medicine. Lissos minted its own coins, one of which depicted the head of Artemis with a dolphin on reverse.

*Grass Hill Poem:*
See *Grass Hill: Poems and Prose by the Japanese Monk Gensei*, translated by Burton Watson (Columbia University Press). Gensei (1623-1668) was a Kyoto monk of the Nichiren sect, a branch of Mahayana Buddhism emphasizing the Lotus Sutra: all people have innate Buddha-nature, and are thus capable of enlightenment in their present lifetime.

*Essential Guantanamo:*
Guantanamo is home to some of Cuba's best roots music. Originally, I had envisioned a poem to celebrate the *changüi*, a rural and working class dance music (guitar with African percussion) played in *aire libre*—as opposed to *puerta cerrada* (closed-door) salon music enjoyed by the upper class. The poem never matured, but what resulted fulfills another aim: to alert the Americano that Guantanamo is not simply GITMO, but a city and a province endowed with a rich culture and vibrant history of *música popular*.

*Blue Guitar, Yellow Wave:*

One morning in Piazza Retonda (opposite the Pantheon, marked with an obelisk from the temple of Isis), a singer—poised Joplinesque, hands at her sides—burst into Leonard Cohen's *Hallelujah*, her unmiked voice magnificently crystalline in the spring air. No doubt the ghost of our trusty bard gave a smile, across the way, over a caffè in the Tazza d'Oro.

John Brandi has been an active walker, writer, visual artist since boy-hood rambles in the mountains of California. He continues to seek source and renewal in his travels abroad and in northern New Mexico, his home for fifty years. In 2015 a limited edition of his Southwest prose poems, *Into the Dream Maze,* was issued by the Press at the Palace of the Governors, Santa Fe, followed by *Planet Pilgrim,* his paean to Japanese poet Nanao Sakaki. He received a Touchstone Distinguished Books Award 2017 for *A House By Itself: Selected Haiku Masaoka Shiki.*

Author photograph: Renée Gregorio

2/20